Alliteration All Around
A to Z

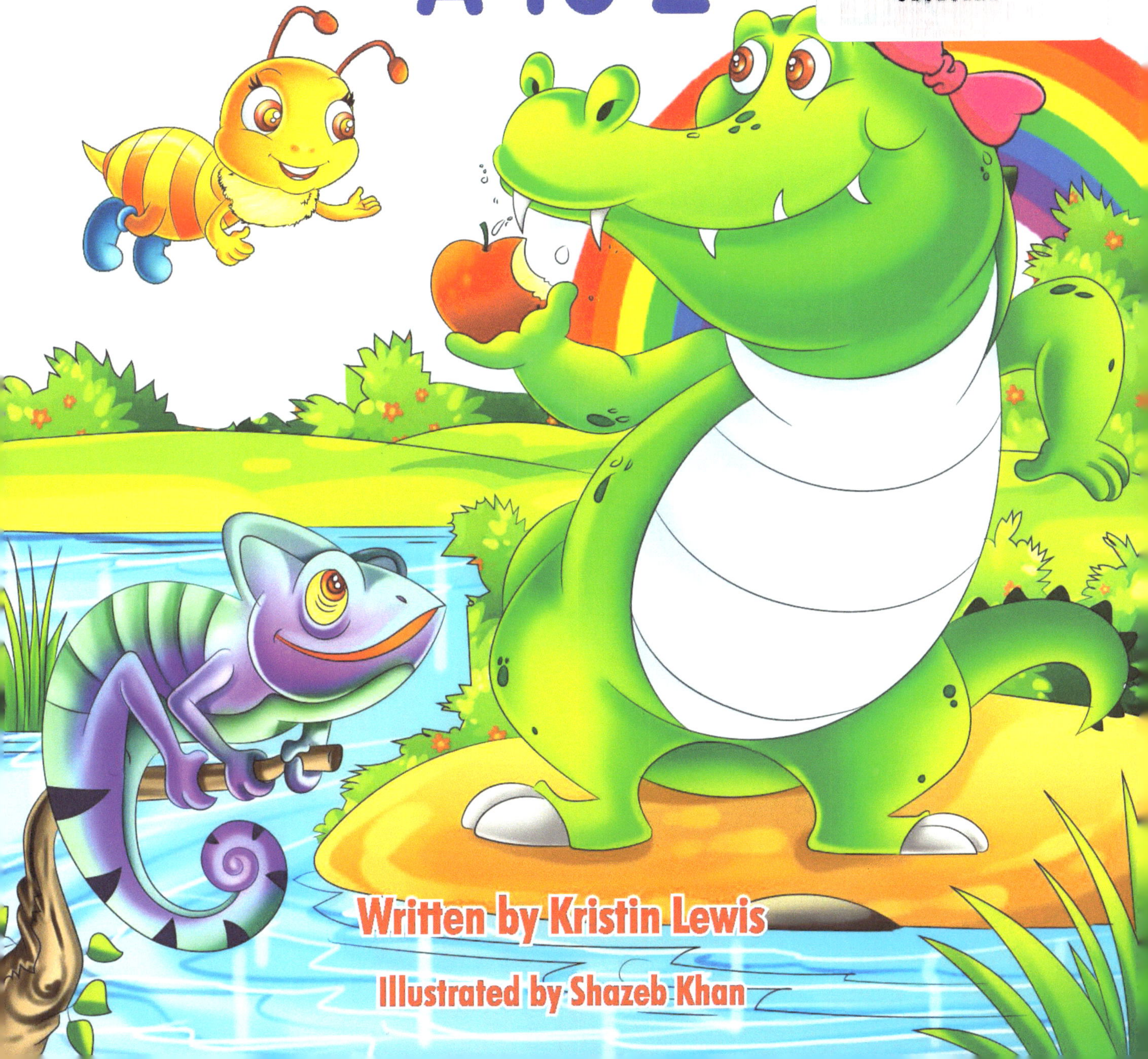

Written by Kristin Lewis

Illustrated by Shazeb Khan

Copyright © 2021 by Kristin Lewis

All rights reserved. No part of this book may be reproduced, distributed, or transmitted in any form or by any means, including photocopying, recording, or other electronic or mechanical methods, without the prior written consent of the copyright owner, except in the case of brief quotation embodied in critical articles, reviews, and certain other noncommercial uses permitted by copyright law.

CARL the chameleon changes colors constantly.

Dolly the dolphin dives all day.

ELLIE the electric eel eagerly eats every day.

FRANK the farmer is friendly to his farm friends.

GROVER the grasshopper grew to be gigantic.

HATTIE the hare hops high and eats honey.

Ivan the iguana irritates Ivy.

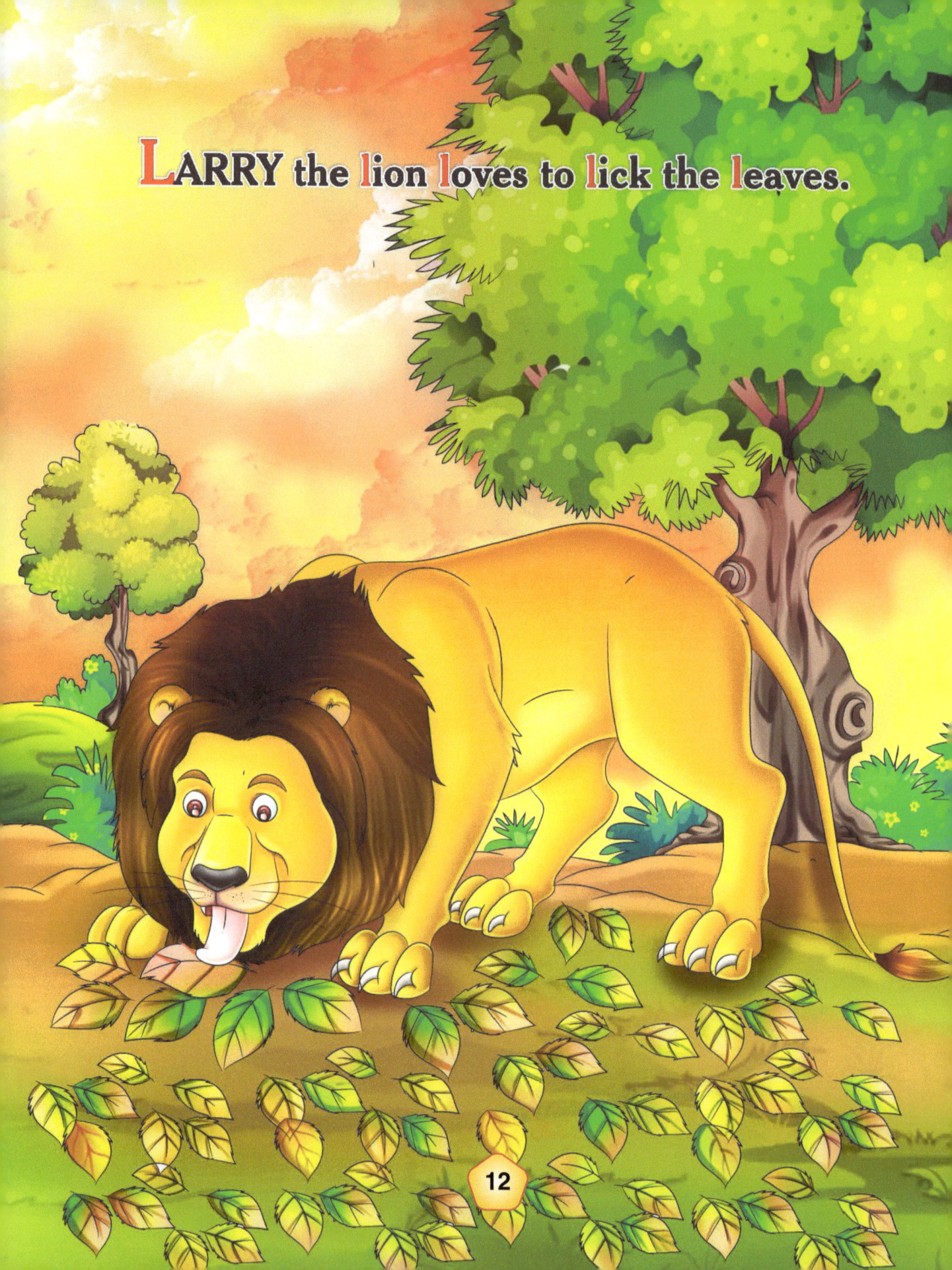

MICAH the mouse moves to the music.

Nora the noisy newt nestles next to Nancy.

OLIVER the octopus obediently opens the olives.

Patrice the pig plays in her pen.

Quennie the quail quietly coos.

Tomar the tiger tosses tires to Tonya.

UNICE the unicorn uniquely makes U-turns.

VIOLA the vulture views the volcano.

XANDER the x-ray fish xeroxes under the expansive sea.

Yanis the yodeler yodels and yells while using her yo-yo.

ABOUT THE AUTHOR

Kristin Lewis Fullenwellen is an author and entrepreneur. Kristin's most recent children's books include: **From the Ashes of Covid: We will Rise, You are Special!** and **What Comes on the Page before me?** To learn more about Kristin and her books and business, follow her on Instagram@Kristhechosen1 or @breakthroughuniversity.

www.ingramcontent.com/pod-product-compliance
Lightning Source LLC
LaVergne TN
LVHW072100070426
835508LV00002B/186